DXB-HI!

FOR ANYONE WITH A
DREAM OF RELOCATION

JAZMINE STEVENSON

For Anthony, the person who taught
me how to overcome relocation fears
and continuously pursue my dreams.

ABOUT THE AUTHOR

Jazmine Stevenson

Jazmine is originally from the UK and has lived in Dubai, United Arab Emirates, for six years; she is a successful entrepreneur running a start-up company Firetap Marketing DXB for Lawfirms and companies in the UAE. She also sits as Business Development Manager and Head of Real Estate & Pro-Bono at local firm Kashwani Law based in Dubai and as Business Development Partner at International firm Spencer West LLP.

Jazmine uses her legal experience and passion for business development to ensure that all her clients achieve their goals when relocating to the UAE. From general legal advice to opening a company or developing a business in the UAE, she works with an advanced team of qualified International Lawyers and marketing professionals to help clients achieve business strategy goals and assist individuals and franchises with advice when working in the UAE to ensure success in the region. Jazmine hopes this book will be a handy guide for anyone, individual or company considering relocation to the UAE and provides essential advice for success in the Emirates.

DXB_HI

TABLE OF
CONTENTS

01

INTRODUCTION

After reading this book, you will be thinking about relocating to Dubai, travelling to the Emirate or become curious about what it is like in Dubai and how expats get by in their day-to-day life! Dubai's increasing popularity, tax-free living and sunshine all year-round, has so many people are asking;

Should I move to Dubai?

Should I relocate my business or open a franchise?

How do I even move to Dubai?

Since moving to Dubai in 2016, I have had many enquiries from colleagues, friends and schoolmates asking about Dubai, what it is like to live here and how to get a job here. I have held online seminars with colleagues from the UK discussing my experiences, and I have also had legal enquires in my field from opening a business in the Emirate to how to move to this dreamy city!

So I decided right... I love talking about Dubai, encouraging people to visit or move here and sharing my experiences, so I have written this short book to answer as many questions as possible for those thinking of coming here! I have put together everything I wish I had known before my relocation, from where to live to what to wear! I have included as much as possible, detailing all of the things I wish I knew before getting on that flight - starting with what to pack!

You can read the entire book in **75 MINUTES!** That's it 75 minutes for everything you need to know before your relocation or skip to the chapter that is relevant to you!

I hope this book becomes a useful tool for anyone who reads it! Quick Facts for skim reading and a referral network of well-recommended people I have personally worked with come with the book! From securing a job to purchasing a property in the Emirates, this handy guide can help you achieve your dreams!

02

MY START!

Six years ago, one of my best friends from university called me, having visited Dubai and said, *"we have to move there - it is amazing and the place for us"* at the time, I was working at an excellent law firm and progressing in my legal career, but the high tax in the UK made it nearly impossible at 25 to save for a house deposit. In addition, the constant rain and de-icing of the car were becoming more and more depressing every morning. That's when I decided to go for it and take the leap and I have not looked back since! I accepted the first commission-only job offered to me, handed in my 3 months' notice, packed up my house, had my leaving party, and stepped onto the flight! Looking back, it seems scary, but the fear completely dissolved once I stepped off that plane and began my new start!

On arrival in Dubai, I was amazed at how big Dubai was! Having looked at pictures, I imagined it to be a tiny road, thinking that the Palm was the whole of Dubai at one stage! Since my relocation, I have not had any regrets. Dubai really **IS** the city of dreams and I have achieved so much in a short space of time, that I truly believe if I had stayed in the UK, I would not have been able to achieve these goals.

From meeting my Husband to becoming Head of Real Estate at Kashwani Law firm, a Business Development Partner at Spencer West London, a CEO of my own start-up company, FireTap Marketing DXB and now a published Author, I can confirm that Dubai really is the city that turns dreams into reality! Although I do have 5 job roles, I still find time for fun and living life to the full in this exciting city.

This guide will help you if you are considering a relocation from who to fly with, where to live and how to make friends - you too can turn your dreams into reality!

From a London, British expat - here are the basics of what you need to know if you are thinking of moving to Dubai!

03

TOP 10 FACTS THAT YOU SHOULD KNOW! (THAT I DID NOT)

01. The President of the UAE is Sheikh Mohammed Bin Zayed Al Nahyan

02. The Prime Minister of the UAE and Ruler of Dubai is Sheikh Mohammed Bin Rashid Al Maktoum

03. The official religion is Islam

04. Dubai's official language is Arabic, but people speak English fluently

05. Dubai has one of the lowest crime rates in the world

06. There are 7 Emirates that form the UAE (**see chapter 6**)

07. Dubai is Tax-Free on all income earnt. **YES, THAT IS TRUE!!**

08. The Currency in Dubai is the Dirham referred to as AED

09. Emmar & Nakheel are two famous developers you will see the name on many buildings in Dubai

10. Haggling is very appropriate, and some stores expect it! You can achieve a bargain price if your skills are good, especially in the Gold Souq & Markets

04

10 TOURIST ATTRACTIONS – MUST VISITS!

01.   Burj Khalifa – At the top or At.mosphere restaurant

02.   Museum of the Future

03.   Dubai Aquarium & Underwater Zoo

04.   Dubai Miracle Garden

05.   Dubai Garden Glow

06.   Dubai Frame

07.   IMG World of Adventure

08.   Gold Souq

09.   Atlantis Water Park

10.   Dubai Desert Quad & Dune Bashing

10 QUICK LEGAL FACTS

01.   Swearing and rude gestures are illegal

02.   Recreational drugs are strictly prohibited

03.   Driving under the influence of alcohol is strictly prohibited

04.   Most employment visas last for 2 years and need to be renewed with the same process each time

05.   You must have a medical to get a valid visa issued

06.   Annual Leave & Holidays – Most companies have a trial period of 6 months probation before you can take a holiday, so be sure to check and confirm this before booking your holidays

07.   Unmarried couples **CAN** live together in Dubai and the UAE

08.   It is not permissible to take photos, record people or record phone conversations unless the consent of the parties is obtained. (You will not see paparazzi here)

09.   You must give written notice to your landlord to move out of your apartment of at least 90 days - you can not just leave at the end of the tenancy without notice

10.   Be respectful of different customs & cultures. You have to remember that there are many different nationalities and you are in a foreign country so always keep that in mind

WHAT ARE THE EMIRATES AND WHO ACTUALLY LIVES IN DUBAI?

When I moved to Dubai in 2016, the population was 2.5 million. Dubai is constantly growing, and the tax-free lifestyle means that the city sees an influx of new people looking to start their Dubai dream each day. Today the population has reached 3.5 million - a massive influx since I first landed in this beautiful city!

The first fact I learnt on arrival in Dubai was that it is linked to 6 other Emirates. I didn't know how big Dubai was or that all of the Emirates were literally united (Duh! United Arab Emirates Jaz!), and all 7 were a short drive away from each other. There are 7 Emirates which make up the United Arab Emirates (UAE), and Dubai is a city within that Emirate. The other cities are Abu Dhabi - the Capital, Sharjah, Ajman, Ras Al Khaimah, Umm Al-Quwain, and Fujairah. All are beautiful cities with their own attributes and expat population, some of which have crystal clear water and are known for their staycations offering scuba diving and all-inclusive weekends away. They are only roughly a 1-2 hour drive away, so you can reach most of these cities and enjoy a weekend away at any time!

The people that live and are born in Dubai and who are citizens of Dubai (**NOT RESIDENTS**) are called Emiratis. The people who emigrate to Dubai from their home country and live and work here are called residents and expatriates.

Expats make up a staggering 89% of the UAE, which means you will meet people from all around the world! People relocate here every single day, making their Dubai dream a reality! It really is an amazing place where you can meet people who speak various languages, with the Emirate incorporating food and events from residents' home countries.

Dubai's official language is Arabic, but most people who live here speak English fluently. Most directions signs and newspapers are written in English and Arabic, so you should have no trouble getting around at all! The official religion is Islam, but other religions are also recognized. There are mosques and churches and **ALL** religions are accepted.

QUICK FACTS

If you are born in Dubai, you do not automatically become an Emirati! Children inherit their parent's nationality dependent on where they are from.

07

JOBS & RECRUITMENT

EMPLOYED

The main question that I am often asked (Even though I am not a recruiter) is either "how do I get a job in Dubai?" or "can you get me a job in Dubai?". New jobs arise every day in Dubai under every single category! For anyone following my socials, I do provide recruiter referrals and info on how to bag your dream role!

One thing to note is that although there are many job roles, competition is rife, and you need to stand out from the crowd to grab that dream role. There are 2 options to obtaining a job: one is to apply from home, secure the role and then move out here, while the second is to arrive on a tourist visa, freelance visa or job seeker's visa and then seek employment while here. From my experience, I believe it is easier to secure a role whilst you are in Dubai - I have literally been to an interview one day and was offered the job on the spot! However, everyone relocating needs to make the right decision based on their finances and liabilities. Most companies offer very good packages, and you will always receive an employment visa and medical insurance from a legitimate employer. They will also never ask for fees upfront, and your employer should always pay for your visa.

For previous job applications, I have found LinkedIn, Reed, Indeed and Recruitment companies really useful in securing my roles, as well as reputation and direct offers on LinkedIn. **Most roles will ask for your qualifications, and you should get these legal documents attested in advance.**

 QUICK FACTS

You must have a Visa to live and work in the Emirates.

You will be given a card called a United Arab Emirates Resident Identity Card – this is a very important document and should be kept on you at all times.

You cannot open a bank account or rent a long-term property without a Visa & EID

SELF – EMPLOYED

Over the last few years, I have received a lot of enquiries at my firm about setting up a business or franchise in the UAE. I have assisted many clients and watched their business journeys and dreams come true, which really is an amazing experience.

The Emirates offer many options for expats to open their own companies, but most people do not know where to start! I can assist with all business enquiries, so feel free to reach out to me directly for further advice!

 QUICK FACTS

Hire a lawyer (even for a free consultation) to discuss your business plan before paying to set up your business.

If you own your own business, you can personally apply for a visa for yourself and your staff members.

If you open a company and a Trade license, you must legally liquidate that company when you wish to close it, you cannot just leave it open, you must stick to the legal process.

When attending interviews in person in the UAE, always aim to arrive early! I have lived here for years and am constantly lost, so head off early to ensure time to find the location, parking and building.

TIME SCALES

If you are looking for a role and finding it takes some time, do not lose hope! It took me 2 years to get my dream role - if I can do it, anyone can! Perseverance is key, and only YOU can make it happen!

You can read the entire book in 75 MINUTES! That's it 75 minutes for everything you need to know before your relocation or skip to the chapter that is relevant to you!

08

OPENING YOUR
OWN BUSINESS

If you decide to open your own business in Dubai or move your current business to Dubai, the opportunities are endless! Firstly, you need to decide what business activity your company comes under - this should be defined by the exact service you are offering. Examples of business activities could be General Trading, Marketing Consultancy, Financial Services, Lawyers and Advocates - you can have multiple activities under one license if approved.

Before opening any business or franchise, you should consult a professional in this field. I have had so many clients waste thousands of pounds on the wrong license and have had so many difficulties opening their companies because they did not seek the correct advice.

After deciding your business category, you will need to decide in which Emirate you want to open your business - there are multiple options across the Emirates. If you plan to open a company in Dubai, you have so many options, from Freezones and DIFC to Mainland. The possibilities are endless, and you will be able to find the perfect solution to make all of your business dreams come true! Some license categories allow 100% foreign ownership, whilst others require a local sponsor.

After a business consultation, you will be able to decide where to open your business and what is the best and most suited option for you. You can then proceed to hire managers, as well as staff to arrange visas for yourself and the team.

VALUE-ADDED TAX (VAT)

A new VAT rule has recently been applied in the UAE; the general VAT rate is 5% and applies to most goods and services. A business must register for VAT once the threshold of 375,000 AED has been achieved. A qualified accountant based in the UAE can advise you on your corporate matters and how to register your business for VAT.

 QUICK FACTS

If you decide to close or abandon your plans, you must **LEGALLY** liquidate the company - leaving a Trade License open can result in fines.

Licenses generally require yearly renewals.

Some Licenses require a physical business address and an EJARI contract, while others allow Flexi- Desks and virtual offices.

Corporate Tax will be applied from June 2023 but freezones are exempt from VAT and Corporate Tax.

09

NETWORKING

Networking is key in Dubai, and I have met so many of my clients via networking events. Online forums offer many events, as well as large conferences at places like the World Trade centre. Every day, there is an event that you could attend to meet new people and potential clients. If you are looking specifically for other Brits, then groups such as the British Business Group and other Facebook groups like Brits in Dubai are the place to start! I carry my business cards with me wherever I go and also send a digital version when exchanging numbers (especially on nights out in case of memory loss!). Even if someone doesn't need your services immediately, they will remember you for future enquiries!

JOB- SEEKING

Networking is a great way to put yourself out there if you are looking for a new job role. Attending events in your sector and adding people on LinkedIn is a fantastic way to meet your future employer!

BUSINESS LUNCH

Networking and meetings are key in Dubai! Most clients want to meet face to face or will want to meet up when they arrive in Dubai. Business lunches are one of my fave things to do mid-week as you can meet your clients in a nice environment and enjoy a yummy lunch! Business lunches are a great way to meet clients, with the lunch menu, offering a fraction of the normal dinner menu cost. Places like Zuma in the DIFC offer a 2-course lunch for 159 AED, making it one of my go-to restaurants, as well as Sushi Samba on the Palm and Maine in the stunning Opus building! There are many offers you can find online, and these can be booked even if you aren't really working - you still have to eat!

10

MAKING NEW FRIENDS

If you are moving to Dubai alone or even with friends or a partner, the whole idea can be very scary - almost terrifying...

However, you'd be pleasantly surprised to hear that making new friends is so easy in Dubai! People will literally come up to you in the street, start talking and invite you out. Dubai is a very friendly city, and as the population is 89% expat, you will find that everyone has been in the same position you have! There are a lot of social pages on Facebook, such as all girls ATB Group and Brits in Dubai, where you can meet with like-minded people who share your interests. People will put up posts saying "is anyone new in Dubai and want to meet for a coffee?" so don't be afraid to put yourself out there! Networking events are also great places to meet like-minded people and source business, so do check online for events that you might be interested in attending as a way to meet new people! Being away from home can be quite lonely at times so try and stay in touch with people from home and your work place and reach out if you are missing family in the groups.

11

FLIGHTS AND TRAVEL

Dubai's airport, Terminal 3 is recorded as the world's largest airport terminal and is a hub for international travel.

Dubai is situated in a great location, and you have access to so many countries around you, making it a great base for those who love to travel! Not only do you have access to the other Emirates, Saudi Arabia and Oman, but you also have countries like the Maldives (a short 3 hours journey away), Turkey (4 hours away) and Zanzibar (only 5 hours away), as well as London - my home town only 7 hours away! Most airlines fly to Dubai, and you can find great deals online.

Emirates, Fly Dubai, Etihad Airline and BA are my go-to airlines. The airport is conveniently 15 mins from my house (gone are those 2-hour drives which should take 30 minutes to London Heathrow). I fly with them as much as possible, and the experience is always amazing from arriving at the airport!

Emirates Airways is based in Dubai, and you can bag loads of freebies by collecting skywards points on everyday spends in the city. Emirates Skywards can be obtained by many outlets in the city, and one of the best ways to redeem those points has to be in my experience at the Dubai Emirates Lounge in Terminal 3! If you are flying with Emirates and have accrued enough points, you can use them to access the lounge, the unlimited food and Moet is the best way to start your travels and, we can all agree that the food tastes even better when it's complimentary!

For those looking for adventure at a bargain price, you check out Wizz Air and Pegasus that fly to and out of Dubai from multiple locations. I personally embarked on a 15-hour Wizz air flight to London once, and despite having to wear all of my clothes, I was most definitely happy with my £100 return ticket! On the other hand, BA also offers a sale once a year with discounted fares, so keep an eye out for those offers!

Booking that first flight is so exciting, whether for travel or relocation! I remember arriving at London Stansted with my 2 cases, saying goodbye while my parents, sister and friends sobbed, acting as if they would never see me again, only to fly out 2 weeks later and see me around 6 times a year! I must add, this was probably more than they did when I lived back home!

If you are starting your relocation dream, you will always remember that moment that you stepped on that plane! That is a core memory moment that you will never forget!

12

VISA PROCESS

There are several different visas that you can obtain. Each individual **MUST HAVE** a visa to live in the Emirates unless you are a local/Emirati. You must undergo a medical process to obtain the visa - there are **NO** exceptions! The medical process can be daunting if you are like me and faint at the sign of a needle, but try not to worry, as the blood test is just a quick pinch and will be over in seconds!

Your employer will typically arrange your visa, and there are a few steps you should be aware of. Please note that the rules can change, but the basics are as follows:

01. You may need to present **ATTESTED** Certificates for the visa application

02. You may need to be physically present in the Emirate and have an entry stamp in your passport (depending on the type of visa)

03. You will need to attend a Medical Apt in the Emirate where your visa is being issued

04. After passing the Medical, you will need your biometrics taken and you will then have to wait for your visa and EID to be issued

05. On receipt of EID, you can open your bank account and rent an apartment!

06. The entire process can take between 2 weeks – 6 weeks so bare this in mind before trying to open an account and rent a property

ATTESTATIONS

You may often hear this word and think, "what is an attestation?". As you can imagine, there are hundreds of colleges and Universities worldwide – therefore, your employer may ask you to attest your qualification documents. This requires making a copy, and taking both the copy and the original to a solicitor or Notary who will confirm that the document is a **True Copy** of the original. Afterwards, you will need an Apostille or stamp from your Embassy/Foreign office confirming the document to be authentic, followed by a stamp from the UAE Embassy in your home country and a final stamp in the UAE. Only then is this document fully attested.

OPENING A BANK ACCOUNT

To open a bank account, you must have a visa, and to open a personal account takes less time and requirements than opening a business bank account.

Business bank accounts require more documentation and can take up to a month to be established.

Credit card and loan applications can be made at a number of banks on receipt of your visa and salary certificate.

In order to apply for credit, you need to have received your salary into a bank, or alternatively provide 3 months of salary statements.

 QUICK FACTS

You may need to get your qualifications attested before applying for your visa. To avoid delays, confirm this with your employer as early as possible during the visa application process. Attesting documents can be a lengthy process involving using a solicitor to certify documents, apostilles and stamps from several embassies. I have assisted many clients with this process, and I've learnt that it's good practice to give yourself at least 3 to 4 weeks to get everything in order and to get the documents back.

ANNUAL LEAVE & PUBLIC HOLIDAYS

Dubai has many holidays, which makes the move here even more exciting! Looking back on last year, I believe I was able to rack up 60 days! Yes, 60 days of annual leave!

The standard rule is that each employee receives 30 days of annual leave. Most people take this in a one-month vacation, travelling back to their home country for the entire month.

You will also receive most of the public holidays, depending on your work sector. There are currently 14 official public holidays in the UAE.

In addition, some companies follow the 4. 5 day working week, which gives you a half-day on Fridays and allows time to attend Holy Prayer at the mosque.

During Ramadan, most companies reduce their hours, and you will also have half days and reduced working hours, depending on your sector.

In total, this gives roughly a staggering 60 days of annual leave combined! Absolutely amazing!

Types of visas:

If you are not taking an employment visa, there are a number of other options for you, from Investment visas to Golden visas, 5-Year Multi-Entry Tourist visas and Business Single Entry. Due to the variety of options, you will usually require a consultation to determine the best one for you!

WHAT IF I DON'T HAVE A JOB YET?

Your visa rules will depend on the country your passport is issued in – this will need to be researched further before visiting the UAE. There are a number of options for you, from a new job exploration visa to a Green visa for Freelancers and a Business Single Entry visa. There are multiple options for you to explore the categories and secure that dream role from inside the Emirate or even open your own business and become your own boss!

13

MEDICAL INSURANCE & HEALTHCARE

HEALTHCARE

Dubai offers access to hundreds of healthcare facilities. If you are employed you will receive mandatory health insurance, if you are self-employed you will need to organize your own insurance and insurance for any of your employees. Each health insurer provides different options and access to different doctors, surgeries and hospitals. You should receive a list of approved medical centres from your insurer. If you wish to consult a doctor from your home country i.e. British, a quick look online will provide you with a list of doctors in various medical practices whom you can contact.

IMPORTANT

You cannot just walk into any hospital/medical centre unless you are willing to pay privately! You will be given an approved list of medical places that you can visit from your insurer. If you see an unapproved facility from your list, you will be required to pay privately.

MEDICATION

When bringing medication into the UAE, you must carry a copy of your doctor's prescription. It is important to note that some medications which are legal in your home country may not be legal here, so it's best to look online at the approved medication list before travelling, you can also reach out to the embassy for further guidance. Pharmacies in the UAE deliver, so you can easily find most of your go-to medications for collection or at-home delivery.

14

SECURED THE JOB.
NOW WHERE TO LIVE?

Having lived here for 6 years, I have moved 17 times so far. Yes, 17 times! I believe that the last time I called my mum and said I was moving again, she nearly put the phone down, asking, "how can you be moving again?!".

The good thing is that Dubai has no shortage of apartments, hotels and places to stay, so you will be spoilt for choice!

The standard process that usually happens when you relocate is to get your visa & EID. You can then open a bank account and apply for a chequebook - rental payments are still made in cheques so you will need that chequebook handy to secure your apartment!

Apartment rentals are typically on a 1-year contract which has to be renewed yearly. The standard renewal notification is 90 Days (3 Months) from the end of the contract. When looking for an apartment, there are many options to consider - from price to location, the world is literally your oyster! There are areas that are known to be hugely populated with British expats, such as the Marina, JLT, Downtown, JVC, Dubai Hills, Sports City and Motor City. Each area has its own charm and provides different amenities.

Prices also range depending on the area you live in, and there are deposit payments required upfront (so make sure you budget for them!). The best way I have found to secure a rental is via a trusted agent on Property Finder. You can also find short-term lets on Booking.com and Airbnb. Some landlords allow sharing, and you can find a room to let on Dubbizle or popular expat Facebook forums.

QUICK FACTS

I would recommend booking a short-stay hotel or apartment on your arrival in Dubai. As you can imagine, the photos you see online are not always accurate and the apartment may not be in an area that is suitable for you or for getting to work, so the best thing to do is either book an interim stay and dedicate a few days to finding somewhere perfect or ask a friend on the ground if they can view on your behalf. You need to feel comfortable on arrival in this new city, and the place you live in is key to success during those first few weeks.

FURNISHED OR UNFURNISHED?

You will come across several options for apartments - some will be empty and require furnishing, while others will be fully furnished. It is your own choice what you choose to go for. If you choose unfurnished, you will find all of the go-to stores for home essentials like IKEA, and you can also find some absolute bargains on expat Facebook forums, including free items! I was able to fully furnish my first apartment for about 1000 AED (Yes, an entire 2-bed apartment), so you can set your budget and then embark on your furniture hunt.

PURCHASING PROPERTY IN DUBAI

If you decide to purchase a property in the UAE then you should always use a trusted RERA approved Real Estate Broker and make sure you do your research before purchasing a completed or off-plan unit. Research is key! As well as deposits and mortgage approvals, it is always important to not overleverage yourself, so speaking with a financial advisor or property lawyer is key before making these big decisions.

Once you have assets in the UAE you should have a Will drafted and registered to protect those assets, there are Muslim & Non-Muslim options here, as well as multiple courts for registration including but not limited to Dubai Courts, DIFC & ADGM. A lawyer will be able to advise you on the best route suited to your needs and to protect your assets as you wish.

— 66 ————————————

Expats make up a staggering 89% of the UAE, which means you will meet people from all around the world! People relocate here every single day, making their Dubai dream a reality! It really is an amazing place where you can meet people who speak various languages, with the Emirate incorporating food and events from residents' home countries.

———————————— 99 —

15

FURRY FRIENDS – CAN I
BRING MY PETS?

Many of my clients have asked what to do about their pets! There are so many furry friends in Dubai and a number of companies that will help you relocate your furry friends. If you are looking to adopt a pet when you arrive here, you will find many shelters with pets looking for good homes! Animal Rescue UAE has many pets that need homes, as well as K9 friends. There are also several places that help with pet care, from mobile grooming to looking after your pets when you are away - you will have everything you need here to make sure your furry friends are spoilt!

 QUICK FACTS

Certain breeds of dogs are prohibited in the UAE. Dog owners must be aware that the United Arab Emirates does not allow all breeds for import, and you will need to make an enquiry before arranging for your furry friend to travel with you.

16

HOW TO PHONE HOME!

| MOBILE NUMBER

The best thing about moving here is sending that message to everyone with your new UAE Number - it finally feels real! There are 3 well known network providers in the UAE - DU, Etisalat and Virgin. All mobile sim cards must be registered, so you can only obtain one with your passport. You will need an Emirates ID to officially register the number and make it permanent, as well as taking out a pay monthly contract.

| TOURIST SIM CARD

Tourists can get a sim card with a copy of their passport and Dubai airport offers some complimentary sim cards on arrival. You can use a monthly pre-paid plan for data and minutes if you do not have your visa yet.

 ———— QUICK FACTS ————

WhatsApp, Facetime and any social media calling platforms do not work in the UAE, but calling home has never been easier! We normally use Zoom and Google Meet for all calls back home and local business meetings. You can also pay a small monthly fee to call with Botim. Most providers offer international packages, and I currently have unlimited UK calling minutes, as well as international minutes, making calling home easier than ever!

17

ALL THE SERIOUS STUFF
– MOVING DAY!

Moving day is either the most exciting or worst day for you, depending on the circumstances!

On my last move, my rescue cat Archie (a huge 15lb Arabian Mau, google the breed – he's massive!) managed to escape from the cat box and claw me, ripping my clothes whilst I was trying to drive! Meanwhile, my husband (sitting in his air-conditioned office) questioned why I was so stressed after he had arranged an all-inclusive moving company... Nevertheless the stress, once the furniture is all in, you feel a great sense of relief and excitement about your new Dubai Pad!

Check this Step-by-Step guide, so you don't get caught out (Like I did) on my first moving day.

01. View apartments with a **TRUSTED** Real Estate Broker with a RERA License number

02. Agree on the final price for the year's rent

03. Pay a deposit to secure the apartment (Deposit is 5% of total rent)

04. Agree on the installment payments – Installments range from 1 Cheque (Full Payment upfront) – 12 Cheques (Monthly)

05. Review the contract and any addendums

06. Sign the contract. The landlord must also sign the rental contract

07. Apply for an EJARI - Mandatory registration of your tenancy contract

08. Apply for a Move-In Permit (Mandatory!)

09. Get the keys!

10. Register with Dubai Electricity & Water Authority (Deposit is required)

11. Register with Gas Authority If GAS is needed (Deposit is required)

12. Register with Chiller (AC) Authority if Chiller is not included (Deposit is required)

13. Register with DU/ETISALAT – Home WIFI/PHONE/TV

14. MOVE-IN!

MOVING OUT

When it comes to moving out, you must give your landlord notice of a minimum of 60-90 days. The tenancy contract will detail how many days' notice you will need to give, and this should be a written notice – NOT VERBAL, sent to the email address detailed in the contract. If you fail to do this, you can risk your tenancy being renewed for another year.

RERA

Whether you couldn't reach an agreement with your landlord or you are the owner of the property and facing legal issues, RERA is the first place to lodge a case. RERA act as an ombudsman to resolve issues, if you cannot resolve the issue with RERA, you will need to seek legal assistance and have a consultation with a lawyer who can provide further advice.

IMPORTANT – STAY WOKE!

STAY WOKE, people! If you are using a broker, make sure they have a valid RERA license number and company brokerage. Do not hand over cash deposits or pay money into an individual's account! Dubai is a super safe city, but you wouldn't hand over cash to randoms in the UK without proper documents, so don't do it here!

> If you are looking for a role and finding it takes some time, do not lose hope! It took me 2 years to get my dream role - if I can do it, anyone can! Perseverance is key, and only YOU can make it happen!

18

GETTING AROUND
PUBLIC TRANSPORT

Ok, so you are all settled into your hotel or apartment, but how are you even going to get to where you need to go in this huge city? Personally, I have used every form of transport in Dubai, starting with a bus from JVC to the Palm Monorail and can say that it is relatively easy to get around!

In the last year, I have even faced my fear of driving and hit the roads! Now, I can say that I find driving so much easier (despite shaking at the wheel for the first 3 months). I found that it is especially useful for nipping around Dubai when you have multiple meetings.

One of the most exciting things about Dubai is that you can even book a Helicopter ride using the UBER app! Yes, I said it - a helicopter! Fancy avoiding the traffic? Head to your nearest helipoint and jump in for a Dubai City tour. Obviously, we can't take the copter every day; whether you are a tourist or a resident, getting around has never been easier - from public to private transport, there are several options available to you:

01. Taxi – Taxis around Dubai are available from RTA Yellow taxis that you can flag down, Uber or the Careem apps. I prefer to use the app even for the RTA option, as new places open every day in Dubai and not every driver knows where they are. I still only know my way home and back after 6 years!

02. Metro – The Dubai Metro runs on two lines and is very affordable. Starting at around 2 AED, you can purchase a NOL card which is similar to an Oyster card or tap-and-go public card. You top up your NOL card and can easily tap between metro stations.

03. Metro Gold - the Metro can get busy at times, and the Metro Gold card can offer you further luxuries. Located at the very front of the carriage, you can get a great view and a seat for those busy times! You can enjoy the ease of getting this card immediately from any ticket office for only AED 25 (including AED 19 e-purse value). Alternative options that suit you can be explored on the RTA website.

04. Hire a car – Car rental is a frequent form of transport here, and you can hire cars for days and months at a time. There are a number of different car hire companies, which usually request a form of ID upfront and a deposit.

05. Dubai Tram - Dubai Tram uses the same NOL card as the Metro and does not charge from Metro to Tram. The line runs from The Walk to Al Sufouh near the Marina.

06. Dubai Monorail - The Monorail connects Palm Jumeirah to the mainland and requires a separate ticket system.

07. RTA Bus - Similar to the Metro, all RTA buses require a NOL card on a tap-and-go system. When you enter the bus, you will need to place your card on these scanners to pay the RTA Dubai bus fare.

If you are a UK national with a **TOURIST** visa and valid driving license, you can hire an insured vehicle and immediately drive.

If you are a UK **RESIDENT** with a visa, you will need to get your driving license converted to a UAE license. Additionally, you will be required to take an eye test and pay a fee to convert the license. You will only be allowed to drive legally once you are issued a UAE license. Some countries accept a direct license conversion, while others require a second driving test in the UAE, depending on where your license is issued. UK driving licenses can be converted immediately. Additionally, you can also take lessons and get a driving license if you don't already have one.

 QUICK FACTS

NOL cards must be valid, in date and have a minimum amount of AED 7.50 for each journey.

Public transport is amazingly clean, and you are not allowed to eat or drink on the Metro.

Men, Take Note – There are women-only carriages! Public transport offers women-only carriages for women and children only! Make sure you are not accidentally in that section, as you could risk receiving a fine.

There are a lot of social pages on Facebook, such as all girls ATB Group and Brits in Dubai, where you can meet with like-minded people who share your interests. People will put up posts saying "is anyone new in Dubai? and want to meet for a coffee?" so don't be afraid to put yourself out there!

19

PRIVATE TRANSPORT

Alongside being able to hire or purchase your own vehicle, there are several private driver options available. I am sure you have seen videos of people driving in Gold Bentleys and Ferraris. Private car hire is easily accessible in Dubai, and many companies provide super car vehicle rentals if you want to cruise around Dubai in luxury.

Careem and Uber offer private Lexus hire and Electric vehicles, and you can also hire a private driver to drive his car or your car anywhere you need to go via a number of tourist websites.

For those who simply do not fancy driving or have work to do in between meetings, there's a great app called Zofeur, that allows you to organize a collection of you and your car from anywhere in Dubai. This service will take you anywhere, with many options available - you're not required to be in the car, as the driver can take your car, collect family and friends, and arrange a drop off at your chosen location. Anything you need can be organized in Dubai to make your day-to-day life easier!

SALIK

Dubai has a system similar to the London Congestion Charge (but much cheaper). As you drive up and down Sheikh Zayed Road, you will see a number of locations. Each time your vehicle passes through a Salik toll point, Dh4 is automatically deducted from your pre-paid Salik toll account. If you purchase or rent your own car, you will need to register for Salik and purchase a tag - the easiest way to do this is at a Petrol station.

HOW TO TOP UP - SALIK APP

You will need to login using a username and Pin Code. You can recharge and top up the balance anytime.

 ───── QUICK FACTS ─────

Rental companies usually ask for a deposit before you can lease a vehicle. When purchasing a car, you will be required to put down an upfront deposit for new and used vehicles if seeking a car loan.

20

HELP! WHAT
DO I PACK?

When packing for Dubai, I made the mistake of throwing out most of my winter clothes and packing loose and covering items, only to discover that I packed absolutely nothing practical or useful for when I arrived! Don't worry, I won't let that happen to any of you!

WHAT TO WEAR

Dubai is a very lenient city, with most people being expats or tourists. There is an idea that you cannot wear bikinis or short dresses, but this is not correct. As I mentioned, the city is very lenient, and pool and beach days are popular attractions for tourists and residents, but beachwear is only for the beach and pool - not for just walking around town. All swimwear is allowed, from Bikinis to full-covered swimsuits, but nudity is not allowed and it is illegal to be nude in a public place, so don't even think about trying to avoid those tan lines!

For nights out and parties, dresses and nightwear are always worn with amazing outfits that can be seen when heading to any nightlife-style venue. Tourist areas are very lenient, and you do not need to worry too much about covering up. Most posh restaurants will require men to wear trousers and shoes and will advise on the dress code when you call to make the booking.

WHAT TO WEAR IN THE WORKPLACE

Each office/business has its own dress code. Some request a uniform or a suit and tie, while others have a more relaxed, jeans and T-shirts approach - it really depends on your environment and your employers' requests. I work at a local law firm, where the staff dress in a professional way, as you would see in any office environment or city law firm. Men wear suits, while women wear smart outfits. Depending on their nationality and preference, the local women wear Burkas and cover their hair according to their choice. Some do, and some choose not to, while other women wear smart skirts, blazers and dresses in the summer.

Sometimes, I find that the AC is so chilly that I have worn a polo neck to the office! When the weather cools down outside, you will be surprised to see that people have seasonal winter wear during the colder seasons, as many of us have climatized. Going from 50 degrees to 25 can feel chilly to those used to the climate, and you'll most definitely see me with a scarf wrapped around my neck in November despite the 30-degree weather!

MOSQUES, RELIGIOUS PLACES, AND MORE RURAL PLACES

When visiting the older parts of Dubai (such as the Gold Souq - one of my fave places to go Christmas shopping because of the scent of Oud and the Gold deals that you can bargain for hours within the stores), the dress code is a little more conservative. There are fewer tourists in the older parts of Dubai, and you want to respect everyone's cultures when heading to these rural and less touristy spots. When visiting the mosque as a tourist, you will be expected to cover up and sometimes cover your hair. The Mosques that allow tourists to visit will provide you with the appropriate clothing if you do not have it.

For Government Buildings, I always dress professionally. You are not expected to cover your hair, but you will be expected to have arms covered – this is the same as if you were visiting any government entity or court in your home country, as you are expected to dress professionally and more conservatively.

Dubai is extremely open-minded, so you really do not need to worry about how to dress, as long as you are comfortable and respectful.

WARM OR COOL CLOTHING

Dubai can be extremely hot in the summer, so you want to have some more breezy outfits and stay hydrated when heading out in the daytime. During the cooler months, it does actually get quite chilly in the evenings; so do not throw out all your scarves and warmer jumpers like I did! Pack a mixture of summer outfits, professional clothes, going-out evening outfits and some jumpers and shawls for the cooler months. Additionally, it can get chilly when you are in the malls and inside in general, as the AC is always on and combating the heat, so I always wear long sleeves inside or keep a handy scarf in my bag for when it gets too cold.

Leggings, Jeans, Shorts, Suits, PJ's! Pack as much as you can, as you will need most of it if you plan to move here permanently due to the different seasons.

21

REALISTIC COST
OF LIVING

I am sure you have seen countless TV shows and Instagram posts of extravagant properties and mansions and I can confirm that these places do exist, but how much does it cost to live here as an average working expat?

The cost of living in Dubai really can vary on what you want to spend and your expectations. Although every apartment looks amazing, you need to ensure you don't overleverage yourself!

Most people rent a short-term let when moving here to get a feel for what area they like and where suits them best. When picking an area, you must consider getting to work, good locations and your social life. If your employer does not provide accommodation, your cost of living can either be budgeted or extravagant, depending on your income and capital liquidity.

Depending on which Emirate you live in and the type of property you stay in, your rent is directly influenced. You can easily find a studio up to 2 beds on the outskirts of town for 20-35,000 AED per year. You can also find 1-bed or 2-bed apartments in Dubai (if you travel a little further out) for 50 - 65,000 AED a year, which is roughly 12,000 – 16,000 GBP per year. In the more popular areas and center of town like downtown, you can stretch to 80,000 -160,000 AED for 1 -2 beds. The rent prices increase and decrease each year, so you have to consider that the rent you agree can increase or decrease the following year. There is also a RERA calculator, which can predict your rent and how much it can be increased or decreased legally when renewing your tenancy contract.

The average bills are relatively affordable, falling between 80 – 300 Great British Pounds a month. This depends on where you live, the size of your household and whether your property is chiller-free (AC included in the rent). These prices of course, do not include luxury rentals and are based on average 1-3 bed apartments.

Chapter 22 gives a rough guide to what you need to budget for when moving to this beautiful city!

22

KEEPING IT REAL – THINGS YOU NEED TO BUDGET FOR

Ok, all the fun stuff aside, we have to get serious now. Reaching goals and dreams does take some planning, and budgeting in advance helps to avoid future disappointments. The last thing we want is to arrive under planned and not prepared!

Here are all the things you may need to budget for, depending on your circumstances!

RENT

Yearly rent – Rent is paid in cheques and the price for the year is agreed upon upfront.

Room only – usually requires a 1-month deposit.

FURNITURE

Unfurnished units require furnishing so make sure to budget for all the items you will need from forks to Fridges!

DEPOSITS

Rent deposit at 5% of the yearly property price e.g. 60,000 AED = 3000 AED Deposit cheque.

DEWA, CHILLER (AC) GAS, WIFI

All require small deposits, and you should pay the bills monthly.

CAR/TRANSPORT

Car rentals start from around 1400 AED on a monthly basis.

Public transport is considerably cheaper, but may or may not be more convenient. If you aren't considering renting a car, you should rent a property with easy access to the Metro and local amenities to avoid spending on taxis.

Car Rental companies will ask for an upfront deposit.

When purchasing a car, you will be required to put down an upfront deposit for new and used vehicles if seeking a car loan. For car loans, most banks require a minimum salary, so look into pre-approval before paying deposits.

SOCIAL ACTIVITIES

Budgeting for socials, gym, sports, and anything else you like to do in your spare time has to be considered. There are many fun things to do in Dubai for every budget, so you shouldn't find it difficult to keep busy regardless of your social budget.

CHILDCARE

There are a number of companies that can assist you by helping you find in-house childcare, from part-time to full-time in-house childcare. From live-in to live out, there is a variety of options, as well as part-time babysitting/Nannies. In addition, there is a number of nurseries that can easily be found close to where you live, teaching your chosen curriculum and language. The fees can vary from nursery to nursery.

When it comes to schooling and childcare, there are several different options available. From nursery to primary/secondary schools, all the way to Universities, Dubai has no shortage of education options.

STUDY

Dubai is known for having one of the best and most extensive variety of curriculums, no matter where you are from. Dubai offers an option to study your home curriculum or any curriculum of your choice! Additionally, there are options to study at multiple universities from pre- to post-graduate studies. Dubai also partners with a number of institutes worldwide, enabling online studying with options to sit the exams in Dubai to avoid travelling solely for the purpose of taking exams. You will be able to find most courses in this city! Fees, once again, vary from each university, as there is no set fee.

LEARNING ARABIC OR ENGLISH

It is good to learn new skills and a new language is always beneficial. Some companies require bilingual speakers, and whilst you don't need to speak Arabic to get around, learning the language certainly helps for your practical skills. There are many private tutors and institutions that can help you learn Arabic or English in the city.

FOOD

Food prices vary, depending on where you eat and your preference. Dubai has amazing offers on food on online delivery platforms, as well as dine-in restaurant offers. You can easily find a nice meal for 20 AED up to 2000 AED - my husband once accidentally spent 200 pounds! Yes, GBP on 2 Prawns, so be careful when going off the menu in fancy restaurants! He is still scarred from that night out!

Depending on what establishment you visit, there is something affordable for everyone. Now, of course, being a Brit, I am always looking for those home comforts, and if you prefer cooking at home, there are a variety of supermarkets from Carrefour, Spinneys, Waitrose and Kibsons. You can easily find most items that you would purchase at home, as well as a number of different restaurants that provide dishes and food from your home country!

If you don't fancy cooking, food delivery has never been more accessible! Gone are the statements of PJS & bed, lights out, and Tesco is closed! Apps such as Deliveroo and Talabat have a variety of offers with discounts 24/7 whenever you need to order something or fancy a midnight snack!

Dubai also offers access to a variety of restaurants from around the world! So far, there has been no cuisine that I haven't been able to find or try! Not only will you be able to find those friday night snacks that you have back home (I recently embarked on a Milky Way and Chicken Kiev mission which was successful), you will also be able to try food and experiences from the other expat communities and a whole world of different cuisines.

 QUICK FACTS

Pork – Pork is not eaten in Muslim culture, and therefore you can only access pork products in certain places. Don't worry, pigs in blankets and bacon sarnies are still available! Some stores have a non-Muslim section selling the products like bacon and sausages, while some restaurants offer pork products.

If you are cooking pork, please remember to be mindful of the people you are living and working with.

If you are starting your relocation dream, you will always remember that moment that you stepped on that plane! That is a core memory moment that you will never forget!

23

ALCOHOL

Ok, so anyone who knows me personally will know that I love a glass of Pinot Grigio! Nothing beats heading home after a long week and sharing a cold glass of wine with my husband, so what are the rules for drinking in Dubai?

Different rules apply for residents and tourists, and you have to be aware of the guidelines!

You cannot just go into a supermarket and purchase alcohol like you can back home. Alcohol is kept separate from food and supermarket establishments and is only available to non-Muslims living in the Emirate. Alcohol is served at most licensed venues, hotels, restaurants, bars and nightclubs and is accessible to adults over 21 years old.

Aside from drinking in restaurants and hotels, alcohol can be purchased for use from the comfort of your own home with an Alcohol license.

In Dubai, the store that sells alcohol is called African + Eastern or MMI. If you are from the UK, the exact equivalent of the store would be an off-license. I don't know if anyone remembers that place called Bargain Booze, but it is pretty similar!

Some restaurants and venues are dry and do not serve alcohol so if you fancy a cold one, double check before setting off.

ALCOHOL FOR TOURISTS

Tourists can easily apply for a 30-day license with their passport and Dubai entry visa stamp. This will allow you to purchase alcohol from the store for consumption at home.

RESIDENTS

Residents with a visa and Emirates ID will need to visit the store and apply for a license; a small yearly fee must be paid, usually redeemable through vouchers.

DUTY-FREE

When you arrive at the airport, you will see some duty-free stores; you can legally purchase 4 litres of alcohol or 24 cans of beer for personal consumption.

 QUICK FACTS

You **CAN** consume alcohol in your home or hotel room.

Do **NOT** drink and drive! The UAE has zero tolerance to drinking under the influence of alcohol, unlike the UK you are not allowed to drink even 1 unit.

It is illegal to drink in the street or a public place in the UAE.

In the UK, Brunch is referred to as a meal between Breakfast and Lunch, but here it has a whole new meaning, and a brunch package can start anytime from 9 am to 9 pm! Brunch happens anytime, anywhere and any day of the week across hundreds of venues.

24

**ALL THE FUN STUFF!
FIRST STOP –
WE'RE GONNA GO
SHOPPING.**

Ok, all the serious stuff over discovering Dubai is the best part of the journey. Whether you're a tourist or moving to Dubai permanently, this is where your adventure begins! I can still remember my first week in Dubai; I wandered past a hotel bar offering a ladies' night in Al Barsha – 5 free drinks for all ladies (I will come to the ladies' nights later on!) I went in and couldn't believe how friendly everyone was there; I met so many expats, all describing places to go and things to do!

I love visiting that establishment as it reminds me how far I've come in the six years I have been here.

SHOPPING

Dubai is known for its variety of shops; you can pretty much find anything that you need here! From the world's biggest mall to home delivery within 2 hours, you have the world at your fingers when you touch down in Dubai! The Dubai Mall is the largest in the world at 12 million sq ft; trust me, this mall is massive and walking from one end takes me over an hour. If you can't find what you are looking for there, it doesn't exist!

The mall contains not only a cinema but an Ice rink, a 5-star hotel, over 120 restaurants and a 10–million-litre tank Dubai Aquarium. As well as all of the shops, you have the Aquarium and Underwater Zoo where you can actually swim with sharks! By the end of this book, I will have tried that experience and will report back, I promise!

Dubai Mall is not the only place to get your shopping fix, with new shopping centres opening up every day, as well as the Mall of the Emirates, Dubai Marina Mall, Nakheel Mall, WAFI Mall, Dubai Outlet Mall, Burjuman, City Centre Mirdiff, City Walk, Dubai Festival City, Ibn Battuta Mall, Mercato Mall & Dragon Mart to name a few. You will find many stores that you have in your home country, and you can also order a variety of items online!

DIAMONDS AND JEWELLERY

We all know that Diamonds are a girl's best friend, and Dubai is known for its Diamonds, Gold and Jewellery and also the perfect place to get a bargain if your haggling skills are good! The tax-free options mean that you can find jewellery at a reasonable price, and if you can haggle well, you can really get a bargain!

The Gold Souq is a known place for lovely pieces, and you can find anything you are looking for, from Gold to Diamonds & Engagement rings. You can find jewellery stores everywhere in Dubai, and some famous places include Dubai Gold & Diamond Park, Dubai Mall and Mall of the Emirates. Dubai Mall and Mall of the Emirates stock designer items like Cartier, Tiffany & Rolex, these luxury stores are all under one roof, and you can find anything you are looking for, no matter the budget.

ONLINE SHOPPING

There are so many online stores in Dubai, and you can literally order an LV bag if you want to (only if you have the spare cash) with a 2-hour delivery! Online stores such as Instashop have various options, from makeup to pens & sellotape. The online platforms can provide you with everything you need!

Food Takeaways & Delivery services take around 30 mins to an hour for home delivery, and food shopping can be done on apps such as Carrefour delivery in only 60 minutes. For last-minute groceries, Talabat delivers to your door in 20 minutes. You can even Whatsapp some stores to arrange delivery, Dubai uses technology to ensure anything you need can be supplied at your convenience with the click of a button!

Careem also offers an incredible facility where the driver will go to any store to collect an item, pay for it and bring it wherever you are! This is a superb service, and I used it for last-minute name tags on my wedding day, an hour before the ceremony! It is an absolute lifesaver.

Dubai is known for its variety of shops; you can pretty much find anything that you need here! From the world's biggest mall to home delivery within 2 hours, you have the world at your fingers when you touch down in Dubai! The Dubai Mall is the largest in the world at 12 million sq ft; trust me, this mall is massive and walking from one end takes me over an hour. If you can't find what you are looking for there, it doesn't exist!

25

HOW DO I GET POST?

HOME DELIVERIES & POST

Ok! So, when I arrived my mum kept asking how she could send my birthday card.

Apartments and houses in Dubai rarely have postcodes. The old way of finding a place would be via description (First house on the left by the Carrefour – no joke!) Now Google maps and Waze can get you anywhere you need to be, but there is NO home postal service, all Post is delivered by Private courier to your home/office, and they will need your address and correct mobile number to find you! I normally use DHL and Aramex as they offer a quick turnaround time of a few days for UK-UAE deliveries.

Emirates Post offers a postal collection service where you can have any items/letters sent to the post office and collect them in person with your ID. You can also pay for a dedicated PO Box where you can have your mail sent and collected in person at your convenience, which is what most businesses have.

QUICK FACTS

Emirates Post centres are dotted around Dubai, so make sure that any letters/items are delivered to the postal office that is closest to you; otherwise, you may face a lengthy drive to the other side of town.

I suggest using a private courier for anything valuable or essential. If you send items from the Emirates Post centre to the UK, it is straightforward and reaches the UK promptly. You will need to provide your ID when sending Post.

PAPERLESS BILLS - All house utilities bills are paperless, so gone are the days of waking up to 20 demand letters on your doormat; they come via email instead, so lost in the post doesn't quite swing it here!

26

SPORTS & FITNESS

Despite being a hot country, Dubai offers a variety of sports! From Tennis to Bike riding through Al Qudra, if you are into sports, you will have no issues finding numerous places to enjoy working out. Horse riding & Equestrian is one of my fave activities, whilst my husband loves the Golf season playing all year round despite the 50-degree summer days!

One of my absolute favourite places to visit is SkiDubai. It features an indoor ski slope, meet the penguins and even a snow cinema; it is always ice cold there, and even during summer, it remains at -1 degree.

There is an abundance of gyms in Dubai, and you really can find anything you need, from Women's only to Disco Gyms and Men's Body Building academies, even a pitch-black gym if you don't like people being able to see you while you get your sweat on, there is something for everyone!

With gyms comes an abundance of PTs, so staying in shape and getting qualified nutritional advice has never been easier! For those that like to compete, you can join popular Facebook pages in Dubai, which seek people to join football teams, badminton teams and all popular group and competition sports. There are also yearly sporting events like bike rides along SZH road and Dubai Fitness Challenge.

For Football, Cricket, and Rugby lovers, most sports bars offer all the live shows, and BEIN sports offers every match from the comfort of your home! Fancy some underwater Yoga? Then head to Atlantis for the weekly aquatic activities. Padel is the newly popular sport here, and Padel spots are popping up everywhere in Dubai as well as Kayaking; there is no end to water sports in Dubai! For those seeking adrenalin and adventure – SkyDive Dubai, QuadBiking and swimming with Sharks in the Dubai Mall Aquarium are just some of the options Dubai has in store. You will be spoilt for choice!

 QUICK FACTS

Most venues are seasonal, so outside sports are less frequent or occur from sunrise/fall during those hot summer months.

27

TIME TO PARTY &
WEEKENDS AWAY

NIGHTLIFE

Dubai's nightlife is second to none! I spent my first six weeks here trying out every venue and ladies' night possible before my heels finally gave up on me and my feet decided to retire! Dubai's nightlife starts in the day, from pool parties to lunchtime brunches leading to after parties and nightclubs; you will never be short of options in this bustling city. Parties, going out, and brunches really are second to none, and you can find anything for any age group and theme. They even have children's brunches for days out with the kids to 9-hour all-inclusive adult brunches; there is something for everyone at any time if you are looking for a party!

RESTAURANTS

For those that prefer dinner options, apps like the Entertainer and DoJoin offer hundreds of 241 deals from breakfast on the 51st floor in the Burj Khalifa to evening brunches; you will never be short of dining options in Dubai. Dubai's multicultural presence means you can find any cuisine here, so don't be shy to try new places!

HOTELS

Dubai offers near to 600 hotel options throughout the Emirate, so you are literally spoilt for choice. Most hotels provide different facilities, so doing a little research before booking is essential. Residents also get reasonable offers if they fancy staying away for the weekend and UAE resident discounts. Some hotels offer great party vibes like the Five Chain, while others are more focused on couples or families. There are some really amazing hotels with everything you need under one roof like Atlantis, The Palm and Atlantis Royal that even showcased a live opening performance from Beyoncé for their grand 2023 opening! There are also so many all-inclusive offers; whatever you are looking for, you can find it here in Dubai!

STAYCATIONS

Dubai is close to the other Emirates, and you can easily book a weekend staycay that feels like a mini holiday in only an hour's drive away.

As well as being able to drive to the other Emirates, Oman and other close countries offer unique weekend getaways, and Emirates holidays provide short stays at a discounted price if you are looking for a bargain.

BRUNCH!

My favourite word! Brunch.

Brunch deserves its own section because it is one of the dining options that makes Dubai so unique! I absolutely love a bargain, and being able to eat and drink limitlessly is right up my street!

In the UK, Brunch is referred to as a meal between Breakfast and Lunch, but here it has a whole new meaning, and a brunch package can start anytime from 9 am to 9 pm! Brunch happens anytime, anywhere and any day of the week across hundreds of venues.

Brunch deals consist of unlimited food and drinks for a specific time period. They can start at a price of around 100 AED up to 500 AED pp. Brunch packages consist of Non-Alcohol and Alcohol packages as well as two-course meals up to unlimited food. Popular party and dining venues dedicate certain days and nights to exclusive brunch packages. Most brunches also offer live entertainment as well as fantastic food and drinks, all at a bargain price; whatever the set fee for Brunch is, it is all you will spend! So, if the Brunch costs 250 AED from 12-4 pm, that is all you will pay no matter how much you eat and drink! I have tried so many venues, and my current go-to place is still STK Dare to Brunch! If you don't know where to try, head to What's On Dubai for all the latest brunch offers!

MUSIC & THEATRE

Dubai Opera offers a selection of shows throughout the year! From Chicago to Riverdance, your favourite shows will be showcased here, so keep an ear out for upcoming events. Coca-Cola Arena and various nightclubs showcase famous celeb performers from JLO to 50 Cent, and there are exciting Live shows that you can attend most days of the week and sites like Platinum list provide all of the tickets. La Perle is one of my favourite shows, I have been around four times so far, and it still amazes me! From death-defying heights to waterfalls, this show has it all and runs all year round, great for adults and children!

28

WHERE THE LADIES AT?

LADIES NIGHTS

Ok! You may or may not have heard about Ladies' nights, but they are awesome! Several bars and restaurants offer deals for women, from free food to unlimited drinks or discounted food and drinks on certain nights, each venue has a different offer, and you can find these online with a click of a button! Venues such as pool days and even salons offer ladies' day deals, so be sure to check out as many as you can if you love a bargain!

HAIR & MAKEUP

I love getting dressed up for events and nights out here and have made it my mission to try several salons and makeup artists!

Pretty Wow and the Salon are popular favourites of mine. Stacey from Pretty Wow did my wedding hair and it looked amazing on the day! As well as Shona Kennedy MUA for fabulous makeovers (she did my wedding makeup whilst I took 100 panicked calls and still kept her cool!) If you are looking for a spa and salon in one, then The Glasshouse by Caroline Brooks is a must visit! Most salons offer nails and anything you are looking for; Tips & Toes is trendy for your gel and acrylic designs and pedicures. There are also online platforms that supply hair, makeup, massages and nails to your door for treatments in the comfort of your own home.

29

FOR THE GENTS

Worry not, guys; there are now several Men's nights offering discounts on food and drinks for you guys!

Venues like Toro Toro offer half-price steaks and discounted drinks, while McGettigan's Madinat has an Auld Fashioned gents' night every Tuesday, offering three drinks for 50 AED!

BARBERS & BEARDS

I know how serious and loyal you guys are to your Barbers and football team, but moving abroad means the team can stay, but the barber has to be new, Sorry! (Unless you can persuade them to come over here with you)

But fear not; there are so many good barbers in Dubai.

If you are looking for British Barbers, then GC Middle east offers a nice list of recommended places and CG Barbershop comes personally recommended by my Husband, "*it is elite,*" so be sure to try them out once you touch down in Dubai.

30

HOME COMFORTS

Being a brit, I focus on the British treats that Dubai offers and literally spent four years hunting down an M&S version of a Chicken Kiev!

Now there are so many options to remind you of home, from traditional roast dinners at Reform Social Grill to late-night kebabs from Charlie Khans Dubai. Everything you need to remind you of your home is on your doorstep!

I recently discovered a store called Park & Shop that delivers right to your doorstep, offering Robinsons, Ribena and Lucozade (I actually ate 4 Milky Ways in a row on discovery!) For general food shopping, you can still access the yummy M&S olives while Waitrose, and Spinneys stock most British products.

If you are looking for clothes stores that you have in the UK then you have everything from M&S to Zara in the Malls and even a Matalan in Burjuman mall. Sadly, we still need a Primark, but I know there is a petition to open a store here!

Fibber Magee's and McGettigan's are places to be if you love Irish pubs and there are a lot of restaurants and bars that offer home comforts, including themed events such as St Paddy's Day. You should easily find anything you are missing from home in this city.

31

RAMADAN &
CHRISTMAS IN DUBAI

RAMADAN IN DUBAI

Ramadan is a Holy month, which lasts between 29, or 30 days, depending on moon phase sightings; during this time, Muslims must abstain from all food or drink from sunrise (fajr) to sunset (maghrib). Ramadan occurs once a year, and during Ramadan, capable Muslims are required to abstain from eating and drinking from dawn to dusk.

In Dubai, non-Muslims are expected to be considerate of the people who are fasting. Once the sun sets, you will hear a large canon, which explodes, marking the symbol of sunset and time for Iftar!

Dubai comes to life in the evening as people break their fasts with an Iftar. Tourists and expats are welcomed and encouraged to join in the celebrations, with many hotels and restaurants hosting elaborately decorated Ramadan tents.

Working hours are often reduced during the daytime, and the end of Ramadan marks a Holy celebration and public holiday for everyone called Eid al-Fitr.

CHRISTMAS IN DUBAI

Dubai goes the extra mile for Christmas, with decorations everywhere along the boulevard and events on Christmas day. Head to Madinat Jumeriah for the Christmas markets, or book a Christmas day brunch to get into the festive spirit!

32

GENERAL INFO
& LEGAL TIPS

Dubai has two Court systems; one is under Sharia/Mainland Law, and the second is under UK Common Law in some Freezones, including the (Dubai International Financial Centre) DIFC. The DIFC Courts are an independent English language common law judiciary.

The Dubai Courts provide not only Sharia rulings but also Non-Muslim rulings for issues such as divorce and probate matters, as well as access to various International and Local Arbitration Courts and dispute centres such as RERA. Dubai Court rulings are all in Arabic, whereas the DIFC Court is conducted in English.

Dubai is a multicultural city and caters to other expats; the two court systems allow access to Sharia and Non-Muslim courts for all residents, depending on the issue that needs to be resolved.

Where your business, job, apartment, etc., is located in Dubai will determine which court has jurisdiction over any legal matters. Contracts signed in Dubai can specifically reference the jurisdiction under which any legal issue should be dealt with, as well as local and international arbitration matters, should they arise. Religion also plays a part in determining which court has jurisdiction to hear and make decisions.

A lawyer can advise further on a case-by-case basis about any matters you may have, suppose you have a matter that falls under Mainland and you cannot speak or read Arabic. In that case, most competent law firms will provide you with a legal translation so that you can understand the case rulings. They will also translate any document or evidence in English into Arabic, so you need not worry about the language barrier.

33

SUPER IMPORTANT!

ARABIC DOCUMENTS

One important fact you must remember is that Dubai is an Arabic-speaking country; all mainland documents, whether it be your employment contract or court documents, will be in Arabic. If you need help understanding a document, you should seek advice from a lawyer or legal translator before signing. An Arabic-speaking friend can also provide a translation, but for anything official, you should have the documents legally translated into English before signing them.

VERY IMPORTANT

BANK ACCOUNTS AND IMPORTANT DOCS

When opening a bank account, setting up your Tenancy contract/ Ejari, and all of your utility bills, make sure you use a dedicated email address to which you will always have access! All of your essential documents will be sent here, and if you lose access, you could face legal implications if you miss important emails or notifications.

VERY VERY IMPORTANT

You must remember that this is a different country, Dubai is so multicultural sometimes that it feels like you are still in the UK, but you have to remember the rules and laws are different here, so you can not just assume things are the same as they are back home. I recently had a client that had opened a company and not closed it down correctly (liquidated), leaving it open for four years, fines had accrued, and he was shocked at the fees and time it would take to resolve the matter, saying it takes 5 minutes to close a company down in the UK at Companies House, seemingly forgetting that this is not the UK!

If you have any enquiries are signing contracts or opening a business in the UAE then please reach out to a lawyer or consultant before making key decisions.

34

SHOULD I STAY OR
SHOULD I GO?
THE FINAL DECISION

For those that are thinking of relocating and are now sold from reading the above, I wish you all the best in your future! Leaving family and friends behind can be daunting, but remember your loved ones and true friends will always stay in touch. For anyone undecided, ask yourself - If this is the best version of you and how much can you achieve with this version of yourself? Relocation doesn't have to be permanent, and even a few months abroad will give you a new experience, life lessons and core memories that can never be erased!

Only you can make that job application!

Only you can book that flight, make that jump and step on that plane!

No one else is going to do it for you!

Moving can feel scary, but it doesn't have to be, and with the tips in this book, you will be just fine! The feeling of pursuing your dreams and achieving your goals is everlasting! Good Luck, People! Nothing is stopping you now!

By Jazmine Stevenson

Should i stay or should i go? The final decision

97

CONTACT JAZMINE

FOR A COMPLIMENTARY CONSULTATION EMAIL:

info@firetap.ae For all Marketing Enquiries

info@kashwanilaw.com for UAE Legal enquires

info@spencer-west.com for UK Legal enquires

This book has been approved to Print by the Ministry of Culture & Youth under Printing Permit number MC-01-018520618, Age Classification E, Hard & Paperback copy published by Amazon ae and Amazon UK.

يجب تدوين رقم موافقة اذن الطباعة و اسم المطبعة و عنوانها بالاضافة للتصنيف العمري مع ذكر الجملة التالية (تم تصنيف و تحديد الفئة العمرية التي تلائم محتوى الكتب وفقا لنظام التصنيف العمري الصادر عن وزارة الثقافة و الشباب) و ذلك للحصول على موافقة التداول

Printed in Great Britain
by Amazon

42621538R00057